How to Debate Your Republican Relatives

Repudiating Trump in the 2016 election

Carl Widell

Dedicated to my Daughters:

Elise, Svetlana, and Katya

and

to my friend, muse and critic

Pamela Heyne

The Promises They Keep

A surprising fact - U.S. president's keep most of their campaign promises. People don't believe this; when promises are made, many feel "it's just a politician talking."[1]

But it is a mistake to disregard campaign promises. Most presidents manage to fulfill the majority of the promises they make. From President Wilson through President Bush over 75% of the promises made on the campaign trail were kept.[2] PolitiFact has tracked all of President Obama's campaign promises and found the he has delivered on 70% of the promises he made during his presidential campaigns.[3]

The press, the candidate's committed supporters, and major donors all press presidents to keep their promises. Donald Trump or Hillary Clinton, if elected, will almost certainly successfully implement most the promises he or she made during their campaigns.

---

[1] Quoted from Timothy Hill, "Trust Us: Politicians Keep Most Of Their Promises." *FiveThirtyEight*, April 21, 2016.

[2] Ezra Klein, "Presidents keep their campaign promises." *The Washington Post,* January 20, 2012. Klein is quoting from Michael Krukones article, "Promises and Performance: Presidential Campaigns as Policy Predictors." *American Political Science Association,* August 1985.

[3] *PolitiFact* as of June, 2016. see: http://www.politifact.com/truth-o-meter/promises/obameter/

Note that a candidate's promises are distinct from the party platform, which is a consensus of policies hammered out by party leaders. Issues on the platform are often ignored by the candidate. As a result, while candidates tend to enact what they promise, they may not enact all of the planks on the party platform.[1]

Many may view Trump, a non-politician, as a special case. Because his promises are often outlandish, his followers feel that he will moderate them once in office.[2] There is no indication whatsoever that this is the case. Any wavering Trump has shown from his originally announced positions has been met with outcries from his supporters. Trump has repeatedly vowed to do what he says he will do.[3]

John McCain and Mitch McConnell have argued that the separation of powers in the Constitution will prevent Trump from doing many of the things he has promised. This may not be true. Eric Posner, a Chicago Law School professor, has examined whether Trump could actually carry out the

---

[1] Suzy Khimm, "Do party platforms really matter?" *The Washington Post*, August 23, 2012.

[2] Jenna Johnson, "Many Trump supporters don't believe his wildest promises — and they don't care." *The Washington Post*, June 7, 2016

[3] Peter Wehner, "The Indelible Stain of Donald Trump." *The New York Times*, June 10, 2016.

policies he has announced and concluded that, for the most part, he could.[1] With Congress' assent, George Bush and Barak Obama have considerably expanded presidential powers over the past fifteen years. Posner concludes that Trump could use these expanded powers to push through the majority of his policies. It follows that we should pay close attention to promises made on the campaign trail by both candidates.

This book does not focus on scandals, such as Clinton's email server or Trump's business bankruptcies. These do not relate to the candidate's promises. It does not focus on issues where the candidate has changed positions so often that his or her current position cannot be viewed as a promise, such as Trump's reversals on social security. It focuses only on campaign promises made during the campaign.

Each issue is presented with quotes from the candidates, followed by a summary of the issue and an analysis of the implications of each candidate's stance. Use the footnotes to delve further into a topic that interests you.

---

[1] Eric Posner, "And if Elected: What President Trump Could or Couldn't Do," *The New York Times,* June 3, 2016.

Remember, the winning candidate will have a strong motivation to keep as many of his or her campaign promises as possible. The press, their opponents, and the prospect of re-election will all hold the new president's feet to the fire. When deciding your vote, it makes sense to look closely at the promises made by each candidate and consider how these policies will affect your life. Focusing on campaign promises is also the most effective way to debate your Republican relatives.

Table of Contents

The Promises They Keep i

JOBS 1

Job Losses to Trade 2

Job Losses to Immigration 7

Job Losses to Technology...10

Job Losses to Currency Manipulation.................................13

The Trans-Pacific Partnership..16

Create Jobs by Rebuilding Infrastructure 19

Create Jobs By Lowering Taxes 22

NATIONAL SECURITY 25

The Islamic State (ISIS) 26

NATO...29

Military Alliances and Nuclear Security.............................32

Cybersecurity 36

Russian Policy 39

Libya 42

IMMIGRATION **46**

Build a Wall..47

Banning Muslim Immigration...51

Mass Deportation or Amnesty?...54

TAXES AND THE ECONOMY..**58**

Taxes..59

Do Tax Cuts Stimulate the Economy?...................................63

Income Inequality and Growth..66

Regulating Big Banks: the Dodd Frank Bill 70

THE SOCIAL SAFETY NET **73**

Food Stamps and Welfare..74

Affordable Care Act (ObamaCare) 79

Planned Parenthood's Federal Funding................................83

Gun Control...86

Student Debt..89

Climate Change..93

Jobs

Job Losses to Trade

Trump: "Chinese trade deals are killing U.S. jobs. We should put a 45% tariff on Chinese goods. The Chinese factories will find it too expensive to sell to the US and American workers can keep their jobs."[1]

Clinton: "We gain as many jobs as we lose with trade. While we must encourage trade and remain an active participant in international growth, we must also protect those workers who are harmed by overseas competition."[2]

The Issue: from 2001 to 2013, 3.2 million U.S. jobs were moved overseas due to lower labor costs. Three quarters of these were in manufacturing, and most of these jobs were lost to China.[3] At the same time, the Department of Commerce states that in 2008 10.3 million jobs were supported by exports, an increase of 2.7 million from 1993.[4] The question is, "How should the US deal with job losses to

---

[1] Reena Flores, "Donald Trump wants huge tariffs on Chinese exports to the US." *CBS News*, January 7, 2016.

[2] See: https://www.hillaryclinton.com/briefing/factsheets/2015/12/07/winning-competition-for-global-manufacturing-jobs/

[3] Katherine Peralta, "Outsourcing to China Cost U.S. 3.2 Million Jobs Since 2001." US News & World Report, Dec. 11, 2014.

[4] *Exports Support American Jobs*, U.S. Department of Commerce

globalization, when we are also generating jobs from trade?"

Trump's Promises. Trump feels we need to renegotiate all of our trade agreements to restore jobs for U.S. workers. Trump proposes a seven step plan, including withdrawal from the TPP, renegotiating the NAFTA trade agreement, renegotiating our trade deals with China, appointing trade negotiators to identify trade violations by foreign countries.[1] He would bring them to the negotiating table by declaring China a currency manipulator (See chapter on 'Currency Manipulation'). His new trade deal would, "put an end to China's illegal export subsidies and lax labor and environmental standards."[2] Trump would also force China to uphold our intellectual property laws.

Trump's proposals assume he can negotiate a better deal with China than we currently have under the World Trade Organization. He wants to hit China with large tariffs to 'even the playing field', but he seems to be unaware that the U.S. is already hitting China with high tariffs. The U.S. Department of Commerce imposed duties of over 500% on

---

[1] William Gallo, "Trump Unveils Jobs Plan, Takes Aim at Clinton." *VOANews*, June 28, 2016.

[2] From Donald Trump's website. see: www.donaldtrump.com/positions/us-china-trade-reform

China, India, Italy, Korea and Taiwan for dumping corrosion-resistant steel on U.S. markets.[1] The U.S. did the same on solar panels, imposing tariffs ranging from 26% to 78%. in 2014.[2]

It is not clear what Trump means with his 45% tariff. It appears he means to slap it on all Chinese products across the board. If this is true, many economists feel that this type of non-specific, across the board tariff could result in a world wide depression.[3]

Even if he does improve our trade deals, it is not clear that this will result in more jobs for US workers if we remain uncompetitive. Trump has made no proposals to directly help workers who have lost their jobs due to globalization.[4]

Clinton's Promises: Clinton's approach to jobs lost to trade is to provide direct relief to those who have been hurt by globalization. This means temporary cash when they are

---

[1] Holly Elliott, "US hits China and others with more steep steel duties." *CNBC*, May 26, 2016.

[2] Diane Cardwell, "U.S. Imposes Steep Tariffs on Chinese Solar Panels." *The New York Times*, December 16, 2014.

[3] Everett Rosenfeld, "Trump trade plans could cause global recession: Experts." *CNBC*, March 10, 2016.

[4] For a scathing critique of Trump's trade policy from a conservative viewpoint, see Scott Lincicome, "Almost Everything Donald Trump Says About Trade With China Is Wrong." *The Federalist*, January 20, 2016.

laid off, tax relief, re-education programs and loans to start entrepreneurial businesses of their own.[1] She does not feel we can turn the clock back and regain jobs lost to overseas competition simply by imposing higher tariffs.

Clinton recognizes that U.S. manufacturers are becoming more competitive. In 2014, the number of manufacturing jobs returned to the U.S. was equivalent to the number leaving.[2] Clinton also proposes to take the gains the US has made in productivity and enhance them. Her program, called the "Manufacturing Renaissance Tax Credit" – is designed to attract new capital, business, and jobs; a zero capital gains option on long-term investments; and relief for renovating, refurbishing, or repurposing plants."[3] If these incentives prove effective, the US will create more manufacturing jobs - in many cases created by businesses started by workers who lost their jobs. Clinton also says that she will renegotiate the TPP to ensure U.S. workers are protected under its provisions.

---

[1] For a detailed look at the Clinton solution see: https://www.hillaryclinton.com/briefing/factsheets/2015/12/07/winning-competition-for-global-manufacturing-jobs/

[2] Dora Mekouar, "Why US Isn't Losing As Many Jobs to China," *Voice of America*, April 20th, 2016.

[3] Dora Mekouar, "Why US Isn't Losing As Many Jobs to China," *Voice of America*, April 20th, 2016..

The Bottom Line: Globalization is a double-edged sword. Clinton's program minimizes the problems created by trade by providing direct relief to workers who have lost their jobs or who cannot find jobs of equivalent pay. She also enhances U.S. competitiveness with programs to encourage entrepreneurship.

Trump's promises to turn back the clock and restore jobs that were lost to 'bad trade deals' makes no sense. It is unrealistic to expect that jobs lost to China years ago will be brought back no matter how well Trump renegotiates U.S. trade deals. Trump's hammer - high tariffs - will cause retaliation which could very likely cause a world wide depression.[1]

---

[1] Everett Rosenfeld, "Trump trade plans could cause global recession: Experts." *CNBC*, March 10, 2016.

Job Losses to Immigration

Trump: "The influx of foreign workers holds down salaries, keeps unemployment high, and makes it difficult for poor and working class Americans – including immigrants themselves and their children – to earn a middle class wage. ..."[1]

Clinton: "Hillary will introduce comprehensive immigration reform with a pathway to full and equal citizenship within her first 100 days in office. It will treat every person with dignity, fix the family visa backlog, uphold the rule of law, protect our borders and national security, and bring millions of hardworking people into the formal economy."[2]

The Issue: Do illegal immigrants take American jobs? Many voters think so, but many economists see the problem differently. By taking jobs that require low level English skills immigrants free native workers to do jobs which require good English skills. The result is more business, hence more jobs, in the entire economy.[3] With an unemployment rate of under 5% immigrants, legal or illegal, are filling jobs the economy needs filled.

---

[1] From donaldtrump.com. See: https://www.donaldjtrump.com/positions/immigration-reform.

[2] For a full description of Clinton's immigration proposals, see::https//www.hillaryclinton.com/issues/immigration-reform/

[3] Art Carden,"Illegal Immigrants Don't Lower Our Wages Or Take Our Jobs." *Forbes*, August 28, 2015

Trump's Promises. Trump has called for removal of all illegal immigrants in his speeches, using an 'deportation force."[1] He promises that their removal will bring back American jobs. But his proposals in writing differ markedly from his speeches. On his website his plan is similar to Senator Kay Bailey Hutchison's 2007 proposal for 'touch and go' documentation. In Trump's program, immigrants must leave the country, but are allowed to apply for a work permit immediately.[2] The immigrant may not even have to physically leave the country. In practice this looks a lot like Clinton's program, or what some call 'amnesty'.[3] Trump misses the point that the U.S. needs these workers in the present economy.

Clinton's Promises: Clinton feels that immigrants, legal or illegal, do not take away jobs and are a net plus to American society. They add vigor, values and intellect to the U.S. workforce. Her intention is to keep them in the

---

[1] Tom LoBianco, "Donald Trump promises 'deportation force' to remove 11 million." CNN, November 12, 2015.

[2] James Petholoukis,"In practice, the Trump deportation plan might look more like a form of amnesty." *American Enterprise Institute*, March 1, 2016.

[3] Marc Thiessen, "Who Knew? Trump favors amnesty for undocumented Immigrants." *Newsweek*, November 17, 2015.

workforce, but upgrade their legal status so they do not have to live in the shadows.

Clinton promises a program to give illegal immigrants a path to full citizenship without having to return to their country of origin within the first hundred days of taking office.[1] This has been called 'amnesty' by her opponents. She also emphasizes assistance to small businesses who often rely on immigrants.[2]

The Bottom Line: Despite the hateful rhetoric of the Trump campaign, his actual immigration policies look very much like Clinton's - a procedure to re-register immigrants and given them the legal right to work in the U.S. Perhaps he realizes that shipping 11 million illegal aliens back to Mexico is just not practical. His supporters, however, are not likely to forget his promises made numerous times in his speeches. This is a central promise of Trump's campaign; if he does not reconcile what he says with what he has written on his website, it could cost him the election.

---

[1] Sarah Ferris, "Clinton maps out the first 100 days." *The Hill*, July 23, 2016.

[2] Clinton's solution is outlined on her webpage: https://www.hillaryclinton.com/briefing/factsheets/2015/12/07/winning-competition-for-global-manufacturing-jobs/

Job Losses to Technology

Trump: "I will get American jobs back by negotiating better deals."[1]

Clinton: "Workers who have lost jobs due to technology need to be retrained so they can participate in the growing economy."[2]

The Issue: The United States has lost 5 million manufacturing jobs since 2000. A significant portion of these losses were due to technology.[3] More U.S. manufacturing jobs are lost due to technological change than to overseas competition, according to Professor Drezner of Tufts University:

> "…while a small fraction of American manufacturing jobs migrated overseas over the past few decades, a far greater fraction of manufacturing jobs simply disappeared and are not coming back."[4]

---

[1] James Pethokoukis, "Donald Trump should shut up about China and start railing against robots." *The Week*, March 10, 2016.

[2] Clinton's solution is outlined on her webpage: https://www.hillaryclinton.com/briefing/factsheets/2015/12/07/winning-competition-for-global-manufacturing-jobs/

[3] Heather Long, "U.S. has lost 5 million manufacturing jobs since 2000." *CNN Money*, March 29, 2016.

[4] Daniel Drezner, "Donald Trump's Big Lie About the Global Economy." *The Washington Post*, August 3, 2015.

When it comes to job losses in the modern economy, the most important issue is how to address changes in the workplace brought about by technology.

Trump's Promises: Trump simply does not address job losses due to technology. "Trump's talk on trade is bluster," says economist Charles Ballard of Michigan State University. "Even if you did what Trump says, you wouldn't reverse the technology, which is a very big part of the picture."[1] When Trump talks of job losses, he talks only about trade.   Most jobs in the U.S. today are lost due to technology, not trade.

Clinton's Promises: Clinton recognizes that more jobs are lost to automation than to trade and that these jobs are not coming back. As with jobs lost to trade, Clinton proposes to help workers who lost their jobs to technology with temporary cash, tax relief, reeducation programs and assistance to start entrepreneurial businesses of their own.[2]

Clinton's focus is to stimulate investment in technology and encourage 'on-shoring' through tax breaks other

---

[1] Heather Long, "U.S. has lost 5 million manufacturing jobs since 2000." *CNN Money*, March 29, 2016.

[2] For a detailed look at the Clinton solution see: https://www.hillaryclinton.com/briefing/factsheets/2015/12/07/winning-competition-for-global-manufacturing-jobs/

government programs.[1] Clinton also proposes to take the gains the US has made in productivity and enhance them. Her program, called the "Manufacturing Renaissance Tax Credit" – is designed to attract new capital, business, and jobs; a zero capital gains option on long-term investments; and relief for renovating, refurbishing, or repurposing plants."[2] If these policies have their desired effect, laid off workers will receive assistance and be encouraged to start their own companies, which would lead to more jobs. The goal is to stimulate small business, rather than give general capital gains tax cuts to all businesses. More jobs are created by small business than by large corporations and small businesses are less likely than corporations to replace workers with robots.

The Bottom Line: Clinton directly addresses job losses due to technology with a well thought-out, paid-for plan. Trump does not recognize job losses to technology as an issue and simply does not address it.

---

[1] See: https://www.hillaryclinton.com/briefing/factsheets/2015/12/07/winning-competition-for-global-manufacturing-jobs/

[2] Ibid.

Job Losses to Currency Manipulation

Trump: "The wanton manipulation of China's currency is robbing Americans of billions of dollars of capital and millions of jobs."[1] "The U.S. Treasury's designation of China as a currency manipulator will force China to the negotiating table.."[2]

Clinton: "I will expand the ways we respond to currency manipulation, to include effective new remedies like duties and tariffs."[3]

The Issue: Many U.S. lawmakers and businessmen believe that China is artificially pegging the yuan to the dollar, which in turn, is undercutting American jobs. They believe that as the strength of the Chinese economy grows in relation to the U.S. economy, the value of the yuan should also grow, in relation to the dollar. By pegging the yuan to the dollar, China counteracts this growth, making their goods artificially less expensive and giving China an advantage in world markets.[4]

---

[1] Matthew Slaughter, "The Myths of China's Currency 'Manipulation." *The Wall Street Journal*, January 8, 2016.

[2] Doug Palmer and Ben Schreckinger, "Trump vows to declare China a currency manipulator on Day One." *Politico*, November 10, 2015.

[3] Robert Schroeder, "Clinton says she'll fight currency manipulation with tariffs." *The Wall Street Journal*, March 4, 2016.

[4] Paul Krugman, "Taking On China." *The New York Times*, March 14, 2010.

Trump's Promises: Trump claims that the US needs a strong negotiator (Trump) to remedy Chinese currency manipulation and restore the yuan to its value in a free floating market. In the words of Trump's web page:

> "We need a president who will not succumb to the financial blackmail of a Communist dictatorship. President Obama's Treasury Department has repeatedly refused to brand China a currency manipulator – a move that would force China to stop these unfair practices or face tough countervailing duties that level the playing field."[1]

Clinton's Promises: Clinton, like Trump, vows to defend the US against currency manipulation, with duties and tariffs, citing China as a key culprit.[2]

The Bottom Line: Currency manipulation, at least by China, is no longer the problem that it once was. Since 2010, due to reforms initiated by the Chinese, the yuan has appreciated 24% against the dollar. The U.S. Department of the Treasury in its latest report to Congress on International economic and Exchange Rate Policies did not declare

---

[1] See: https://www.donaldjtrump.com/positions/us-china-trade-reform

[2] Robert Schroeder, "Clinton says she'll fight currency manipulation with tariffs." *MarketWatch*, March 4, 2016.

China a 'currency manipulator."[1]   Ten years ago, China's artificial support of the yuan did give Chinese exports an advantage.   Due to international pressure, especially from the Obama Administration, China has allowed to yuan to rise to its natural market level.

---

[1] "2016 U.S.-China Strategic and Economic Dialogue U.S. Fact Sheet – Economic Track", U.S. *Department of the Treasury* press release, June 7, 2016.
.

The Trans-Pacific Partnership

Trump: "The Trans-Pacific Partnership "was designed for China to come in, as they always do, through the back door and totally take advantage of everyone."[1]

Clinton: I don't believe it (the TPP) going to meet the high bar I have set."[2]

The Issue: The Trans-Pacific Partnership is a trade agreement between 12 countries around the Pacific rim. They include the US, Australia, Canada, Chile, Japan, Malaysia, Mexico, New Zealand, Peru, Singapore, Vietnam and Brunei. China is not included and the TPP is in fact a response to Chinese efforts to create its own trade bloc in East Asia. The TPP is designed to reduce tariffs, coordinate regulations, and to improve legal protections on drugs, copyrights, labor rights, and to support efforts to fight climate change. It provides a legal mechanism to reduce

---

[1] Donald Trump on Tuesday, November 10th, 2015 in the fourth GOP primary debate.

[2] As quoted in an interview with Judy Woodruff, pbs.org, October 7, 2015.

disputes.[1] President Obama says the TPP is good for business and will create jobs. Neither candidate agrees.

Trump's Promises. Trump, when he made the statement quoted above, did not seem to know that China is not a part of the TPP. In fact, the TPP was created to, among other things, lessen the influence of China on the East Asia region. Trump later changed his position stating that although China was not a part of the TPP, it ended up benefiting China. PolitiFact, a website run by the conservative *Tampa Bay Times*, carefully studied whether China could gain in anyway from the TPP, and concluded that it could not.[2] Trump has not been specific on why he opposes the TPP or how he intends to fix it.

Clinton's Promises: Clinton, who voted to allow President Obama fast track authority to negotiate the TPP, changed her position during her presidential campaign due to its perceived bias against labor. Her problem is with its investor-state, dispute-settlement chapter (ISDS). While corporations are able to raise disputes under this rule, workers, unions, consumers, communities and other

---

[1] See: http://www.politifact.com/truth-o-meter/statements/2015/nov/12/donald-trump/trump-says-china-will-take-advantage-trans-pacific/

[2] See: http://www.politifact.com/truth-o-meter/statements/2015/nov/12/donald-trump/trump-says-china-will-take-advantage-trans-pacific/

stakeholders are not.[1] Clinton has said she will withhold her approval of the TPP, which could mean a veto if she becomes president, unless the ISDS provision is changed to provide labor and other stakeholders a fair resolution process.

The Bottom Line: Clinton and Trump would veto the current TPP in its current form. Clinton seems amenable to approving the TPP if the ISIS clause is revised. President Obama, however, is still firmly in favor of the TPP as are most Congressional Republicans and a majority of Congressional Democrats.[2] It is probable that Obama will move to pass the TPP after the November election before he leaves office in January.

---

[1] Lance Compa, "How to Make the Trans-Pacific Partnership Work for Workers and Communities." *The Nation*, January 14, 2016.

[2] See: https://www.whitehouse.gov/issues/economy/trade

Create Jobs by Rebuilding Infrastructure

> **Trump:** "If we do what we have to do correctly, we can create the biggest economic boom in this country since the New Deal..... It's a no brainer."[1]

> **Clinton:** " ... the heart of my plan will be the biggest investment in American infrastructure in decades, including establishing an infrastructure bank that will bring private sector dollars off the sidelines and put them to work there."[2]

The Issue: America's infrastructure is in dire need of repair. To bring America's infrastructure up to 'acceptable standards' will cost $3.6 trillion according to the American Society of Civil Engineers.[3] Any proposal to address the entire scope of the problem will almost certainly explode the deficit.

In the budget deal worked out in December of 2015, President Obama and Speaker Ryan settled on a $350

---

[1] The Republican Nominee Is Campaigning on a Trillion-Dollar Infrastructure Plan That He Likens to the New Deal," Eric Levitz, New York Magazine, May 5, 2016.

[2] See: https://www.hillaryclinton.com/issues/fixing-americas-infrastructure/

[3] See The American Society of Civil Engineers website: http://www.infrastructurereportcard.org/executive-summary/

billion package to address infrastructure which was paid for by savings and tax increases.[1]

Trump's Promises: Trump's is proposing a "trillion-dollar rebuilding plan."[2] to create 13 million jobs and prove a major stimulant to the US economy.[3] He likens his plan to Roosevelt's New Deal. Trump justifies his plan on a calculation done by Moody's where it estimated that for every $1 dollar spent on infrastructure for highways and public schools, it would generate $1.44 back to the economy.[4] In fact, since he has proposed no similar spending cuts, Trump would add over a trillion dollars to the debt.

Clinton's Promises: Clintons is proposing a direct investment of $274 billion coupled with a $25 billion Infrastructure Bank.[5] She also calls for reauthorizing the Build America Bonds Program to provide additional funds

---

[1] Russell Berman, "A Major Infrastructure Bill Clears Congress." *The Atlantic*, December 4, 2016.

[2] Eric Levitz, "The Republican Nominee Is Campaigning on a Trillion-Dollar Infrastructure Plan That He Likens to the New Deal." *New York Magazine*, May 5, 2016.

[3] Ibid.

[4] Ibid.

[5] See: https://www.hillaryclinton.com/issues/infrastructure/

for infrastructure investment. Clinton's plan is more likely to win Congressional approval because she has found ways to pay for it. Clinton estimates that her program would create 3.9 million jobs.[1]

The Bottom Line: Clinton has a carefully thought out plan to create jobs and rebuild infrastructure, which is paid for and likely to win Congressional approval. Trump's plan has no details, and while it would also create jobs and build infrastructure, it would greatly increase the federal debt.

---

[1] See: https://www.hillaryclinton.com/issues/infrastructure/

Create Jobs By Lowering Taxes

Trump: "I am proposing an across-the-board income tax reduction, especially for middle-income Americans. This will lead to millions of new good-paying jobs."[1]

Clinton: "It's outrageous that multi-millionaires and billionaires are allowed to play by a different set of rules than hardworking families, especially when it comes to paying their fair share of taxes."[2]

The Issue: Tax cuts can put dollars in people's pockets., but jobs will be created only if people spend their tax savings. The majority of the wealthy put tax savings in the bank, so tax cuts to the wealthy do not have a stimulus effect. Because the U.S. economy is largely a consumer economy, it follows that tax cuts to the middle and lower classes will spur economic growth and create jobs, while tax cuts to the wealthy will not.[3]

Trump's Promises: Trump's tax proposal gives the largest tax breaks for the rich, which limits its value as a stimulus. It is also costly, as he has proposed no budget

[1] "An America First Economic Plan", at DonaldTrump.com

[2] Quoted from her speech on January 11, 2016. See: https://www.hillaryclinton.com/issues/a-fair-tax-system/

[3] Pedro Nicolai da Costa, "Tax Cuts Boost Jobs, Just Not When Targeted at Rich." *The Wall Street Journal*, April 20, 2015.

cuts to offset his tax reduction. It will add as much as $24.5 trillion to the national debt over the coming 20 years in its present form.[1]

Clinton's Promises: Clinton links taxes and job creation by reapplying increased tax revenues obtained from the very wealthy to infrastructure and other programs intended to create jobs. Clinton's tax proposals fall into four categories: (1) Creating a 'Fair Tax Surcharge' which is a 4% tax on all making over $5 million per year, (2) closing tax loopholes created for the very rich, such as the 'carried interest rate' which gives a break to hedge fund managers, (3) restoring the estate tax to 2009 levels, and (4) implementing the Buffet Rule which says the wealthy cannot be taxed at less than the middle class.[2] Clinton intends to use the revenue produced by these tax increases to invest in infrastructure jobs and programs to help small business.[3]

---

[1] Eric Pianin, "Trump's Tax Cuts Would Add $24.5 Trillion to the Debt." *The Fiscal Times*, December 23, 2015

[2] For more details on Clinton's tax plans see: "Investing in America by Restoring Basic Fairness to Our Tax Code.", at https://www.hillaryclinton.com/briefing/factsheets/2016/01/12/investing-in-america-by-restoring-basic-fairness-to-our-tax-code/

[3] See; "Fixing America's infrastructure," and "Hillary Clinton Aims to be the "Small Business President." at https://www.hillaryclinton.com/issues/.

The Bottom Line: Clinton's tax proposals are off-setting. She pays for cuts to the middle and lower class by increasing taxes on the very wealthy. They are designed to be budget neutral. She uses the proceeds from her tax increases to pay for programs aimed at creating jobs.

Trump gives himself and others like him a large tax break, adding to the over $20 trillion to the debt over ten years. With an emphasis on tax cuts for the wealthy, Trump's plan would only stimulate the economy slightly and create few jobs.

National Security

The Islamic State (ISIS)

Trump: "We really have no choice. We have to knock out ISIS," he said. "I would listen to the generals, but I'm hearing numbers of 20,000 to 30,000."[1]

Clinton: "We are in a contest of ideas with an ideology of hate - and we have to win it. I propose a three part plan to combat ISIS."[2]

The Issue: The Islamic State (ISIS), an offshoot of Osama bin Ladin's Al Qaeda, has captured an area originally the size of the United Kingdom in northern Syria and western Iraq. President Obama has determined that ISIS poses a threat to the United States, but not a sufficient threat to commit large numbers of ground troops. He is also mindful of the need to govern Syria once the battle is over, an occupation that most Americans are against and that would cost trillions of dollars.[3]

---

[1] Nicole Gaouette and Barbara Starr, "Trump is calling for 30,000 troops. Would that defeat ISIS?" *CNN*, March 11, 2016.

[2] https://www.hillaryclinton.com/feed/hillary-clinton-just-outlined-plan-defeat-isis-and-global-terror-3-things-you-need-know/

[3] Kristina Wong, "Poll: Americans want more action against ISIS, but oppose ground troops." *The Hill*, November 16, 2015.

Trump's Promises: Trump feels we must commit at least 30,000 troops to beat ISIS, but the Pentagon doubts that is enough. To support 30,000 combat troops we would need an additional 60,000 troops in support roles, and there is a question whether 90,000 soldiers would be sufficient. Once defeated, there is the question as to who would govern the captured territory.[1] No military authority has supported Trump's plan. Even if Trump were successful with his military campaign, he would have a problem of holding what he has taken.[2]

Clinton's Promises: Clinton promises to build on and expand Obama's campaign against ISIS. Few realize how successful Obama has been over the last 18 months. ISIS has lost 40% of its territory and a great number of its key leaders.[3] Clinton proposes a three part plan to capitalize on Obama's successes: (1) Intensify the air campaign to take out ISIS strongholds, leaders and infrastructure, (2) dismantle the ISIS global financial and propaganda network

---

[1] Gordon Lubold, "Retiring Army General Challenges Trump's ISIS Plan." *The Wall Street Journal*, August 12, 2016.

[2] Nicole Gaouette and Barbara Starr, "Trump is calling for 30,000 troops. Would that defeat ISIS?" *CNN*, March 11, 2016.

[3] Jim Michaels,"ISIS loses 45 percent of territory in Iraq, 20 percent in Syria." *USA Today*, May 18, 2016.

by arresting local enablers, blocking money transfers, and promoting opposing propaganda, (3) harden our defenses at home to prevent domestic attacks.[1]

The Bottom Line: Clinton's proposals build on and go beyond President Obama's strategy. She has the backing of numerous generals, including four star Marine Corps General John Allen.[2]

Trump's ISIS proposal has serious drawbacks and has not been endorsed by any military expert.

---

[1]https://www.hillaryclinton.com/feed/hillary-clinton-just-outlined-plan-defeat-isis-and-global-terror-3-things-you-need-know/

[2] Tyler Pager,"Gen. John Allen backs Clinton in hawkish rebuke of Trump." *Politico*, July 28, 2016.

NATO

Trump: "NATO is costing us a fortune and yes, we're protecting Europe with NATO but we're spending a lot of money.....I would send assistance only if they have fulfilled their obligations to us."[1]

Clinton: "Our European allies stood with us on 9/11. It's time to return the favor."[2]

The Issue: NATO successfully stopped the spread of the Soviet Union during the Cold War and in fact many former Soviet states are now NATO members. Trump maintains that the U.S. is paying too much for an alliance that benefits others more than the U.S. While all NATO members meet their commitments under the NATO budget, some NATO nations fall short of the 2% of GDP that they have pledged for defense. As a result there is an over-reliance within NATO on the United States for essential capabilities such as intelligence, surveillance, air to air

---

[1] Glenn Kessler, "Trump's claim that the U.S. pays the 'lion's share' for NATO." *The Washington Post, March 30, 2016.* Also see Vivian Salama, *"Trump hedges on NATO protection against Russian aggression." The Washington Post*, July 21, 2016.

[2] "US Election 2016: Clinton condemns Trump's plans for Nato," *BBC News*, March 23, 2016.

refueling, ballistic missile defense and electronic warfare.[1] The U.S. spends 3.6% of its GDP on defense, and the United Kingdom spends 2%, but Germany spends only 1.2%, France spends 1.8%, Turkey spends 1.7%, Canada spends 1% and Italy spends about 1%.[2]   Should the U.S. put pressure on other NATO members to pay up?

Trump's Promises: Trump would renegotiate the NATO budget to force NATO partners to pay more for their own defense.   Trump was more specific with the Baltic nations. He said that, if these countries were invaded by Russia, he would consider sending military assistance only if they "have fulfilled their obligations to us."[3]   This statement create real concern among our allies and was seen by many in the U.S. and Europe as a break a major break in U.S. policy of the past 60 years.[4]   It may also be out of date.

---

[1] Glenn Kessler, "Trump's claim that the U.S. pays the 'lion's share' for NATO." *The Washington Post, March 30, 2016.*

[2] Ivan Kottasova, "Which NATO members are falling short on military spending?" *CNN Money*, April 15, 2016.

[3] Vivian Salama, "Trump hedges on NATO protection against Russian aggression." *The Washington Post*, July212, 2016.

[4] Ibid.

Recently, thanks to Russia's aggression in the Ukraine, all NATO members have increased their military expenditures.[1]

Clinton's Promises: Clinton supports NATO and would continue with Obama's policies. Clinton has said, "The United States, obviously, has a great interest in helping to maintain peace and security in Europe, and we have a formal alliance, NATO, to do so."[2] Clinton feels the alliance is essential to stability in Europe and our obligations under the alliance are separate from who is paying what.

The Bottom Line: While Clinton makes clear she would continue to support NATO, Trump is suggesting a radical change to U.S. foreign policy. Trump's views on NATO have set off a firestorm of criticism. By refusing to give unconditional support to our NATO allies, Trump would encourage Vladimir Putin in his aggressive behavior in Europe and encourage others to build a nuclear arsenal to defend themselves.[3] Europe would be much less secure if Trump were to enact his promised policies.

---

[1] Vivian Salama, "Trump hedges on NATO protection against Russian aggression." *The Washington Post*, July212, 2016..

[2] Taken from Brainy Quotes. See: http://www.brainyquote.com/quotes/keywords/nato.html

[3] Jeffery Goldberg, "It's Official: Hillary Clinton Is Running Against Vladimir Putin." *The Atlantic*, July 21, 2016.

Military Alliances and Nuclear Security

Trump: "I think we should allow South Korea [and Saudi Arabia and Japan] to have nuclear weapons to defend themselves…More nations are going to get the nuclear bomb anyway."[1]

Clinton: "A President Clinton would likely continue efforts on nuclear security, seek opportunities to reengage on arms control with Russia, and take a tough or tougher line with Iran and North Korea."[2]

The Issue: It has been the policy of the United States over the past 50 years, under both Republican and Democratic administrations, to restrict the number of countries which possess nuclear weapons as a means of making nuclear war less likely. This is the basis of the Nuclear Weapons Non-Proliferation Treaty, the Comprehensive Nuclear Test Ban Treaty, and the Nuclear Suppliers Group, which limits the spread of nuclear materials.[3] Under these treaties, the United States has been quite successful in limiting the spread of nuclear

---

[1] Maggie Habermas and David Sanger, "Donald Trump Expounds." *The New York Times,* March 26, 2016.

[2] Rachel Whitlark, "Where Will the next president stand on nuclear weapons?" *Bulletin of the Atomic Scientists*, May 3, 2016.

[3] Gene Gerzhoy and Nick Miller, "Donald Trump thinks more countries should have nuclear weapons." *The Washington Post*, April 6, 2016.

weapons.[1] Tied to these treaties are military alliances, with Japan and the ASEAN nations in East Asia, with Saudi Arabia and Israel in the Middle East and with NATO in Europe, which guarantee member countries protection under the nuclear umbrella of the United States. Under these treaties a nuclear attack on allies of the United States are guaranteed nuclear retaliation from the United States against the aggressor nation. These interlocking treaties are largely responsible for 'pax Americana', the fact that no nuclear war, or no war at all, has broken out among major powers for 70 years.

Trump's Promises: Trump maintains that the United States does more than its share to protect the security of its allies, and that we can no longer afford it. He feels that Japan, Saudi Arabia, and South Korea, should develop their own military capabilities, even if it means developing nuclear weapons. As Trump put it, ""If Japan had that nuclear threat, I'm not sure that would be a bad thing for us."[2] Trump does not seem to understand that our military alliances with Japan, South Korea and Saudi Arabia are in

---

[1] Gene Gerzhoy and Nick Miller, "Donald Trump thinks more countries should have nuclear weapons." *The Washington Post*, April 6, 2016..

[2] Rachel Whitlark, "Where Will the next president stand on nuclear weapons?" *Bulletin of the Atomic Scientists*, May 3, 2016.

place partly to prevent these countries from developing nuclear arsenals of their own.[1] It has been US policy that more nuclear weapons means a higher likelihood that a nuclear war or a nuclear accident will take place. Trump's policies would increase that likelihood.[2]

Clinton's Promises: Clinton has pledged to continue the policies of the Obama Administration and to uphold all of the treaties cited above to contain the spread of nuclear weapons.[3] She has supported these and other initiatives to limit the spread of nuclear weapons through her career in the Senate and as Secretary of State.[4]

The Bottom Line: Trump's proposals are a radical departure from the treaties put in place by both Republican and Democratic administrations over past 50 years. In the eyes of most experts, Trump's policies would increase that likelihood of nuclear war.[5] His proposals would likely open

---

[1] Gene Gerzhoy and Nick Miller, "Donald Trump thinks more countries should have nuclear weapons." *The Washington Post*, April 6, 2016..

[2] Ibid.

[3] Rachel Whitlark, "Where Will the next president stand on nuclear weapons?" *Bulletin of the Atomic Scientists*, May 3, 2016.

[4] Ibid.

[5] Ibid.

the door for China to be more aggressive in the Asian sphere and Russia to be more aggressive in the European sphere. The world would become a much more dangerous place.

Clinton's policies would continue the nuclear non-proliferation and security policies of the Obama, Bush, Clinton, G.H.W. Bush, Reagan, Carter, Ford and Nixon administrations over the past 50 years. These alliances are essential to stability in the modern world.

Cybersecurity

Trump: "First off, we're so obsolete in cyber. We're the ones that sort of were very much involved with the creation, but we're so obsolete, we just seem to be toyed with by so many different countries, already.[1]

Clinton: "We have to be operating on both of these levels [official and non-official], making it very clear to Russia, to China, that not only that what their government does through various entities, but also if they outsource the work to hackers, they will pay a price." [2]

The Issue: Cyber attacks include stealing protected information from corporate or government websites, flooding a computer's link to web to effectively shut down its operation (denial of service attacks), or interfering with a computer's operations to attack a facility or service. Examples include: (1) the loss of the names, telephone numbers and personal information of State Department officials by the United Cyber Caliphate (ISIS); (2) the defacement of Indian, Chinese and Israeli corporate websites by the Pakistani Cyber Army; and (3) the

---

[1] Cory Bennet, "Trump: US cyber powers so obsolete." *The Hill*, March 28, 2016.

[2] Katie Bo Williams, "Clinton: Cybersecurity will be challenge for next president," *The Hill*, February 3, 2016.

interruption of service of certain US banks believed to be initiated by Iran and North Korea.

While strong measures are needed to prevent interception of data and the hacking of sensitive sites, private is also a major concern. The FBI and Apple Computer locked horns in a famous controversy over access to personal information stored on the iPhone used by one of the terrorists in the San Bernardino massacre. The government ordered Apple to hand over the key to unlock the iPhone. Apple refused. Trump sided with the FBI and Clinton seemed to come down on the side of consumer privacy.[1] The question is, "How do you establish the proper protections needed to defend against cyber attacks while at the same time provide the privacy protections guaranteed by democracies world wide.

Trump's Promises: Trumps assertion that the United States is "so obsolete in cyber" is regarded by most experts as incorrect. The US is widely regarded as the most advanced nation both in its cyber protection and in

---

[1] Jimmy H. Koo,"Will Obama's Successor Carry on Cybersecurity Mission?" *Bloomberg Law*, March 28, 2016.

launching cyber attacks.[1] Trump however has no specific plans on how he would deal with this problem.

Clinton's Promises: President Obama has taken this problem seriously and has appointed a Federal Chief Information Officer (formerly known as Administrator for E-government).[2] He has also reached an agreement with Chinese President Xi condemning cyber hacking. Hillary Clinton has pledged to follow Obama's precedent on this issue.[3]

The Bottom Line: While Trump has identified a serious issue, it is unclear what he intends to do about it. Clinton has pledged to continue Obama's detailed programs on cybersecurity, including a cybersecurity czar and an extensive cybersecurity auditing program for all government agencies.[4]

---

[1] Cory Bennet, "Trump: US cyber powers so obsolete," *The Hill*, March 28, 2016.

[2] "Federal Chief Information Officer," *Wikipedia*, June 29, 2016

[3] Katie Bo Williams, "Clinton: Cybersecurity will be challenge for next president." *The Hill*, February 3, 2016.

[4] Jimmy H. Koo,"Will Obama's Successor Carry on Cybersecurity Mission?" *Bloomberg Law*, March 28, 2016.

Russian Policy

Trump: "'Every time there is friction between United States and Russia, it's bad for both countries. For the people to benefit, this should be fixed. We should be friends."[1]

Clinton: "We have to do more to get back talking about how to we try to confine, contain, deter Russian aggression in Europe and beyond."[2]

The Issue: Russia has challenged the United States in several areas over the last five years, including the annexation of Crimea, the invasion of eastern Ukraine, and the support of President Assad in Syria. The Obama Administration has countered by imposing strong economic sanctions on Russia which have hurt its economy.[3] What will the next president do to curtail Putin's ambitions?

Trump's Promises. Trump, whether knowingly or not, is supporting policies which delight Putin. Trump has praised Putin as a great leader and Putin retuned the

---

[1] Tom Hamburger, Rosalind S. Helderman and Michael Birnbaum,"Inside Trump's financial ties to Russia and his unusual flattery of Vladimir Putin." *The Washington Pos*t, June 17, 2016.

[2] Damien Sharkov, "Where do Hillary Clinton and Donald Trump Stand On Russia?" August 5, 2016.

[3] Michael Birnbaum, "A year into a conflict with Russia, are sanctions working?" *The Washington Post*, March 27, 2015.

compliment.[1] Representatives of the Trump campaign removed wording in Republican Party Platform advocating U.S. supply lethal aid to the Ukraine to protect it from Russian attack. Trump has questioned the U.S. commitment to its NATO allies, something very much in Putin's interest (See Chapter on "NATO").   Trump's former campaign manager, Paul Manafort, was found to have close ties to Viktor Vanukovych, the Putin backed former president of the Ukraine. Manafort's partner was found to be a former Russian intelligence agent.[2] All of these items are troubling in themselves; taken together one must question why Trump is pro-Russian to the detriment of U.S. interests.

Clinton's Promises: Clinton has reaffirmed her commitment to the economic sanctions imposed on Russia for invading Crimea and Ukraine's provinces of Donetsk and Luhansk. Clinton also wants to go further than the current administration by sending lethal aid to the Ukraine, including sophisticated weapons systems and arms. She has also

---

[1] Jeremy Diamond, "Donald Trump lavishes praise on 'leader' Putin," *CNN*, December 18, 2016.

[2] Andrew Kramer, Mike Mcintyre and Barry Miller, "Secret Ledger in Ukraine Lists Cash for Donald Trump's Campaign Chief." *The New York Times*, August 14, 2016.

reaffirmed her commitment to NATO.[1] She is committed to opposing Putin wherever necessary, while keeping U.S. options open for negotiated settlements.

The Bottom Line: Clinton has confronted Putin as Secretary of State and is committed to opposing Russian expansion. She will keep in place Obama's policies and expand on them.[2]

Trump's positions undermine U.S. policy and make us less secure. Michael McFaul, former ambassador to Russia said Trump's policies "makes everyone I talk to around the world nervous - and it makes me nervous." David J. Kramer, former Deputy Assistant Secretary of State under George W. Bush, said he was "appalled" by Trump's comments.[3]

---

[1] Damien Sharkov, "Where do Hillary Clinton and Donald Trump Stand On Russia?" August 5, 2016.

[2] Ibid.

[3] Ibid.

Libya

Trump: ""Now, we should go in. We should stop this guy [Qaddafi], which would be very easy and very quick. We could do it surgically, stop him from doing it and save these lives."[1]

Clinton: We offered the Libyan government a lot of help, which they found difficult to accept. There has been a democratic election. We should not give up on Libya.[2]

The Issue: In February of 2011, when Muammar Qaddafi's tank column was approaching Benghazi, the Obama Administration, spurred on by Secretary of State Hillary Clinton, made a decision to intervene. Together with allies, the U.S. bombed the tank column and saved thousands of lives. Democratic elections were held and a new government was formed. The new democratic government had insufficient control over most of Libya and jihadists trained by ISIS and al-Qaeda took over parts of the country, killing and beheading their enemies as they went.

Complicating matters, the U.S. ambassador to Libya, Christopher Stevens, was killed while organizing a trade

---

[1] David A. Graham. "Trump's Libya Quagmire." *The Atlantic*, June 6, 2016.

[2] Scott Shane as interviewed by Nermeen Shaikh, "The Libya Gamble: Inside Hillary Clinton's Push for War & the Making of a Failed State." *Democracy Now*, March 3, 2016.

outreach program in Benghazi. Republicans have laid the blame for his death at the feet of Clinton, who was Secretary of State at the time. The Senate and the House have issued reports on exactly what happened in Benghazi, and concluded that Clinton was not directly responsible. The report stated that the Pentagon had no military assets which could have arrived in time to protect Ambassador Stevens and that available intelligence provided sufficient warning that Benghazi was dangerous to the point that Stevens should not have gone to Benghazi in the first place. Secretary Clinton had already implemented the bulk of the suggestions on how to improve security from both committees by the time of the reports.[1]

As of August, 2016, the country is in sections; the democratic government controls the east from Benghazi, and various clans of jihadists control Tripoli. The city of Sirte had become a base for ISIS, but as of this writing, ISIS

---

[1] See: "Senate Intelligence Committee Releases Declassified Bipartisan Report on Benghazi Terrorist Attacks." *Press release of Intelligence Committee*, January 15, 2014. and "Select Committee on Benghazi Releases Final Report, Urges Obama Administration to Declassify as Much Information as Possible" at https://benghazi.house.gov/news/press-releases

has been forced out of Sirte, by Libyan government forces aided by U.S. airstrikes.[1]

Trump Promises: Trump has attacked Clinton for using force to defend Benghazi in the 2016 campaign. Because he has switched sides on this issue, it is unclear what he would have done had it been his decision. He has little experience in foreign affairs and often confuses his facts.[2] Trump would likely commit large numbers of troops to the Middle East much in the manner of President Bush.[3]

Clinton Promises: Clinton stands by her decision to use force to protect civilians in Benghazi in 2011. She does not see Libya as a failure but as a work in progress and feels that we need to deepen our commitment to Libya and the Middle East.[4]

The Bottom Line: Clinton has long experience in dealing with crises in the Middle East. She would use more

---

[1] Chris Stephen in Tunis and Ewen MacAskill in London, Spencer Ackerman in New York, "US launches airstrikes against Isis in Libya." *The Guardian*, August 1, 2016.

[2] "Trump's Attack on Clinton's Character," *FactCheck.org,* June 22, 2016

[3] Nicole Gaouette and Barbara Starr, "Trump is calling for 30,000 troops. Would that defeat ISIS?" *CNN*, March 11, 2016.

[4] Kim Ghattas,"Hillary Clinton Has No Regrets About Libya." *Foreign Policy*, April 14, 2016.

force than Obama has, but will not commit large land forces to the region. She is committed to working with the local government to build an effective indigenous government.

Trump's would have to back up his tough talk with a major commitment to ground troops in Libya. Even his plan was successful, he would have to deal with the problem of managing Libya after he he invaded. This would put the U.S. in charge of Iraq and Afghanistan, as well as Libya. It is something we should avoid.

Immigration

Build a Wall

Trump: "I will build a great, great wall on our southern border. And I will have Mexico pay for that wall."[1]

Clinton: "I think all of us on this stage agree that we need comprehensive immigration reform with a path to citizenship. Border security has always been a part of that debate. And it is a fact that the net immigration from Mexico and South has basically zeroed out."[2]

The Issue: Trump maintains that illegal Mexican immigrants are taking U.S. jobs, contributing to crime in U.S. cities, and receiving tax payer funded benefits such as healthcare. To address these issues, Trump proposes to build a wall stretching across the Mexican border to keep illegal immigrants out of the country.[3] Will a wall keep make our border more secure? Or would it be a giant boondoggle accomplishing little? Would revamping immigration policies make more sense?

---

[1] Quoted from Trump's presidential announcement speech, June 16, 2015.

[2] Quoted in 'On The Issues' website (http://www.ontheissues.org/2016/Hillary_Clinton_Immigration.htm) from the 2015 CBS Democratic primary debate in Iowa, Nov 14, 2015.

[3] See "Immigration reform the will make America great again," at https://www.donaldjtrump.com/positions/immigration-reform.

Trump's Promises: Trump's position paper on his wall states:

> "The cost of building a permanent border wall pales mightily in comparison to what American taxpayers spend every single year on dealing with the fallout of illegal immigration on their communities, schools and unemployment offices."[1]

Trump promises to build wall of pre-cast concrete rising to 30 or 40 feet high, covering about 1,200 miles of the 2,000 mile border with Mexico. (Natural barriers can be used for the other 800 miles.) Trump estimates this will cost between $5 billion to $25 billion. He plans to freeze reparations, that total $24 billion, from illegal Mexican immigrants (money sent home to help families back in Mexico) as a way to force Mexico to pay for the wall.[2]

Clinton's Promises. Clinton points out that President Obama has already strengthened the U.S. border with Mexico and has significantly reduce illegal immigration.[3]

---

[1] See "Immigration reform the will make America great again," at https://www.donaldjtrump.com/positions/immigration-reform.

[2] For a comprehensive explanation of Trump's plans see: Miriam Valverde, "How Trump plans to build a wall along the Mexican border." *Politifact*, July 26, 2016.

[3] Stephen Dinan, "Hillary Clinton says U.S.-Mexico border is now secure." *The Washington Times*, March 17, 2016

Clinton says that while the solution is comprehensive immigration reform that would provide a path to citizenship for those immigrants, both Mexican and otherwise, who wish to remain in the U.S., she has supported President Obama in his strong efforts to control the border.

The Bottom Line: Trump's initial premises are false. Mexicans are not responsible for more crimes than natural born citizens.[1] Mexican workers do not take American jobs (our unemployment rate is under 5%), and actually increase American wages.[2] Mexicans who are not U.S. citizens do pay payroll taxes, but do not qualify for benefits, as most states require citizenship papers before benefits are given.[3]

Furthermore, more Mexicans left the US than entered in 2014. There was a net loss of 240,000 immigrants from Mexico in 2014.[4] Although *The Conservative Review* points out that these trends were reversed in 2015, showing a net

---

[1] Michelle Ye Hee Lee, "Donald Trump's false comments connecting Mexican immigrants and crime." *Fact Checker, The Washington Post*, July 8, 2015.

[2] Art Carden, "Illegal Immigrants Don't Lower Our Wages Or Take Our Jobs." *Forbes*, August 28, 2015.

[3] Angie Drobnic Holan,"Fact Checking Immigration." *Politifact*, July 1, 2012.

[4] Julia Preston, "More Mexican Immigrants Leaving U.S. Than Entering, Report Finds." *The New York Times*, November 19, 2015.

migration into the U.S., the immigration from Mexico is not as severe as Trump asserts.[1]

It is also not clear that Trump's wall would actually reduce immigration. The Israeli company that built the wall in Israel says the border could be secured but Trump's wall "is not the way to go." They recommend watch towers and sensors, which the U.S. government is already using in vulnerable areas. Trump's ideas play well to the crowd, but it is not at all clear that his wall would be an effective stop to illegal immigration even if it were built.

---

[1] Daniel Horowitz, "Appallingly Dishonest Pew Study on Immigration Trend from Mexico." *The Conservative Review,* November 22nd, 2015.

Banning Muslim Immigration

Trump: "When I am elected, I will suspend immigration from areas of the world when there is a proven history of terrorism against the U.S., Europe or our allies, until we understand how to end these threats."[1]

Clinton: "I will introduce legislation for comprehensive immigration reform that includes a path to citizenship."[2]

The Issue: Terrorist attacks in the United States, Europe and the Middle East have made voters more fearful. To minimize the threat from terrorist attacks Trump has called for increased scrutiny on any immigrants coming into the U.S., including a total ban on Muslims from certain countries. Others say that, while we should be vigilant - US. background checks are the most stringent in the world and sometimes take two years - we cannot compromise our values. [3] They contend that a ban on Muslims could violate First Amendment rights on religion.

---

[1] Beth Reinhard and Damian Paletta, "Donald Trump Back-Pedals on Banning Muslims From U.S." *The Wall Street Journal*, June 28, 2016.

[2] From speech to the League of United Latin American Citizens (LULAC), July 14, 2016.

[3] Everett Rosenfeld, "How America's screening of Syrian refugees works." *CNBC*, November 17, 2015. Gives details on the screening process.

Trump's Promises: While Trump originally called for a ban on all Muslims entering the U.S., he revised his position in the face of intense criticism. His policy director, Steve Miller, characterized his new position as follows:

> "The best way to prevent continued radicalization from developing inside America is to suspend temporarily immigration from regions that have been a major source for terrorists and their supporters coming to the U.S."[1]

There is still criticism of Trump's new stance. For example, it is not clear that immigrants from France would be banned, a country with which the U.S. has had cordial relations for over 200 years.

Clinton's Promises: Clinton feels that the U.S. must rely on Muslim countries to fight terrorists.[2] She says that Trump's policies, "will make that harder." She points out that we need to build trust with Muslim communities in the U.S. - an important source of intelligence for law enforcement countering home grown terrorists. Trump's words, Clinton maintains, "are already a recruiting tool" for ISIS, and her last point is that Trump is turning Americans

---

[1] Beth Reinhard and Damian Paletta, "Donald Trump Back-Pedals on Banning Muslims From U.S." *The Wall Street Journal*, June 28, 2016.

[2] Clinton's points are from a speech given to a rally in Pittsburgh on June 14, 2016 as quoted in "Read Hillary Clinton's Speech Criticizing Donald Trump's Muslim Ban," by Ryan Teague Beckwith, *Time*, June 14, 2016.

against Americans. What we need, Clinton says, is for everyone to work together to confront Islamic terrorists.

The Bottom Line: Trump's proposals have met with heavy criticism from experienced policy makers, but have met with enthusiasm from the crowds which come to see him speak. Trump gives no specifics, so it is difficult to see how he could make his program work in practice.

Clinton's proposals have been met with praise by Middle Eastern experts.[1]

---

[1] "Clinton's Comprehensive ISIS Strategy Has Drawn Broad Praise", *The Briefing*, HilloryClinton.com. See: https://www.hillaryclinton.com/briefing/factchecks/2016/02/11/clintons-comprehensive-isis-strategy-has-drawn-broad-praise/

Mass Deportation or Amnesty?

Trump: "I would get people [illegal aliens] out and then have an expedited way of getting them back into the country so they can be legal.... A lot of these people are helping us ... and sometimes it's jobs a citizen of the United States doesn't want to do. I want to move 'em out, and we're going to move 'em back in and let them be legal."[1]

Clinton: We should provide a way for these people to become naturalized citizens.[2]

The Issue: There are an estimated 11 million illegal aliens residing in the United States today.[3] Most hispanic Americans who have come to the United States have worked hard and obeyed the law, even if many did stay in this country illegally. Many of these 'illegal' immigrants are employed in small businesses that would be hurt if their employees were suddenly removed. Since many of the owners of these businesses tend to vote Republican, this issue is not always a winner for Republican candidates. So the question is how do you process these unauthorized

---

[1] James Pethokoukis, "In practice, the Trump deportation plan might look more like a form of amnesty." *AEIdeas*, March 1, 2016.

[2] Stephan Dinan, "Hillary Clinton vows to expand Obama amnesty." *The Washington Times*, May 5, 2015.

[3] Jens Manuel Krogstad and Jeffrey S. Passel, "5 facts about illegal immigration in the U.S." *Pew Research Center*, November 19, 2015.

immigrants to ensure they are good citizens and follow the law without a massive deportation costing billions of dollars.

Trump's Promises. Although Trump has called for removal of all alien immigrants in his speeches, and has ranted against their unsavory affect on American society, his proposals in writing are similar to Senator Kay Bailey Hutchison's proposal for 'touch and go' documentation she put forth in 2007. The American Enterprise Institute's James Pethokoukis has quoted Marc Thiessen as saying:

> The fact is, Trump won't need a "deportation force" or an "Operation Wetback" to get illegal immigrants to go home — because he has promised that they can return quickly with legal status. … Under his plan, illegal aliens don't have to go to the end of the line behind those who have complied with our immigration laws. They get an "expedited way of getting them back into the country so they can be legal."[1]

This proposal could end up being a kind of amnesty in that it is a method for registering illegal aliens without making them go "to the back" of the immigration line.[2]

Clinton's Promises: Clinton comes down on the side of those who say that immigrants, legal or illegal, are a net

---

[1] James Pethokoukis, "In practice, the Trump deportation plan might look more like a form of amnesty." *AEIdeas*, March 1, 2016.

[2] Marc Thiessen, "Who Knew? Trump favors amnesty for undocumented Immigrants." *Newsweek*, November 17, 2015.

plus to American society.   They add vigor, values and intellect to the U.S. workforce. Her intention is to keep them in the workforce, but upgrade their status so they do not have to live in the shadows.

Clinton proposes a straight forward program to give illegal immigrants a path to full citizenship with having to return to their country of origin. She pledges to treat every person with dignity while following the law and protecting national security. This is on her to do list for her first 100 days in office.[1]

The Bottom Line: Clinton's proposals have support on both sides of the aisle in Congress. They make sense and she has a reasonable chance of getting a comprehensive immigration bill passed.

Trump has gone out of his way to disparage immigrants, especially immigrants from Mexico.   He claims they hurt American workers, cause crime and calls for their mass deportation. But when his policies are examined - the ones on his campaign website - a different story emerges. Trump's actual proposal is a form of what the conservatives call 'amnesty'.   This duplicity will not sit well with his

---

[1] Quoted from https://www.hillaryclinton.com/issues/immigration-reform/

supporters who expect him to do what he has promised in his speeches.

Taxes and the Economy

Taxes

Trump: "While Hillary Clinton plans a massive, and I mean massive, tax increase, I have proposed the largest tax reduction of any candidate who has run for president this year, Democrat or Republican."[1]

Clinton: "I want to make sure the wealthy pay their fair share, which they have not been doing. I want the Buffett Rule to be in effect, where millionaires have to pay 30 percent tax rates instead of 10 percent to nothing in some cases. I want to make sure we rein in the excessive use of political power to feather the nest and support the super wealthy. I also want to create jobs and I want to be a partner with the private sector. I'm particularly keen on creating jobs in small business."[2]

The Issue: Tax proposals have multiple effects. Reducing taxes will boost the economy; increasing taxes will slow it down. Reducing taxes will increase the national debt; increasing taxes will reduce the debt. Of course these policies must be coordinated with appropriate spending policies for these outcomes to take effect.

There is also the issue of fairness. When 90% of the new income in the last fifteen years has gone to those who

---

[1] Donald Trump in his acceptance speech at the Republican National Convention as quoted by Louis Jacobson in *PoliticFact,* July 21, 2016.

[2] Source: 2015 ABC/WMUR Democratic primary debate in N.H. , Dec 19, 2015, as quoted in *On The Issues*. See: http://www.ontheissues.org/2016/ Hillary_Clinton_Tax_Reform.htm

have the top 1% of earnings (See 'Income Inequality and Growth'), many question whether the current system is fair.[1]

The challenge is to put together changes to the tax system which further a candidate's goals while causing as little damage elsewhere as possible. Clinton and Trump approach taxes in very different ways providing a stark choice between them.

Trump's Promises: Trump proposes large tax cuts to stimulate the economy and create jobs. Most analysts agree that his cuts would stimulate the economy to some degree, but given Trump's current proposals for spending, they estimate Trump's plan would increase the U.S. Debt by $10 trillion over 10 years. This estimate does not take into account massive spending programs which Trump has proposed but for which he has not yet suggested ways to pay for them.[2]

---

[1] The average income for the top 1% went up during this persons from $871,100 in 2009 to $968,999 in 2013. The average wage for the bottom 99% fell from $44,000 to 43,900. Wolfers is talking about pretax income, so income from social Security and other government programs is not included, but this is the result of our current 'free market' system. See Justin Wolfers, "The Gains From the Economic Recovery Are Still Limited to the Top One Percent." *The New York Times*, January 27, 2015.

[2] Leonard E. Burman, James R. Nunns, Jeffrey Rohaly, "An Analysis of Donald Trump's Tax Plan." *Tax Policy Center*, December 22, 2016. Note that Trump revised his plan in August, 2016, which would lower the potential deficit. At the time of publication the details of his new plan had not been fully disclosed.

Trump does not address the issue of income inequality. Because he biases his tax cuts to the rich, Trump minimizes the stimulus affect he might have (see 'Do Tax Cuts Stimulate the Economy'). Trump's proposals do simplify the tax code, making it more efficient and eliminating loopholes and complication in the current code.[1]

Clinton's Promises: Clinton proposes to raise taxes on the rich while leaving taxes on the rest of the taxpayers unchanged. She points out that these higher taxes on the rich will not hurt economic growth. (See 'Do Tax Cuts Stimulate the Economy'). By making the tax code more progressive, she attempts to address the issue of income inequality. Clinton closes loopholes which make it easy for the wealthy to avoid tax on foreign income, and eliminates subsidies for fossils fuels, again increasing revenue and making the system more fair.[2]

Clinton's tax proposals would substantially reduce federal debt, $1.2 trillion over the next ten years, while providing only modest stimulus for the U.S. economy. (Her

---

[1] Alan Cole, "Details and Analysis of Donald Trump's Tax Plan." *Tax Foundation*, September 29, 2015.

[2] Richard C. Auxier, Leonard E. Burman, James R. Nunns, Jeffrey Rohaly, "An Analysis of Hillary Clinton's Tax Proposals." *Tax Policy Center*, March 3, 2016

proposals on infrastructure spending were not in this analysis.)[1]

The Bottom Line: Trump's promises a major tax cut, heavily biased towards the wealthy which will explode U.S. debt by $10 trillion over 10 years. His tax program will produce some stimulus, but it might create more robots than jobs (See "Job Losses to Technology").

Clinton policies are intended to address U.S. income inequality by increasing taxes on the rich and using that money to invest in creating jobs. It would also substantially reduce U.S. debt by $10 trillion over 10 years.

---

[1] For in-depth analyses of Clinton's tax proposals from a liberal point of view, see Richard C. Auxier, Leonard E. Burman, James R. Nunns, Jeffrey Rohaly, "An Analysis of Hillary Clinton's Tax Proposals." *Tax Policy Center*, March 3, 2016. From a conservative point of view, see Kyle Pomerleau, Michael Schuyler, "Details and Analysis of Hillary Clinton's Tax Proposals." *Tax Foundation,* January 26, 2016.

Do Tax Cuts Stimulate the Economy?

Trump: "..his policy proposals, including his tax plan, his recommendations for regulatory overhauls and his call for boosting the domestic energy industry, would push growth to 4 percent annually."[1]

Clinton: "Tax cuts to the wealthy do not stimulate the economy, but tax cuts to the middle class and lower class do."[2]

The Issue: While tax cuts stimulate the economy, tax cuts to the wealthy do not. Only tax cuts to the middle class stimulus the economy because they spend their tax savings almost immediately. Two-thirds of the U.S. economy is consumer based, so putting money into the hands of those who will spend it, stimulates the economy. Putting more money into the hands of the wealthy does not.[3]

Trump's Promises: Trump proposes a series of tax cuts with the largest going to the top 10% of taxpayers. This

---

[1] Lynnley Browning, "Clinton could have cut her tax bill in half under Trump's plan." *Chicago Tribune*, August 21, 2016.

[2] Patricia Cohen, "What Could Raising Taxes on the 1% Do? Surprising Amounts." *The New York Times*, October 16, 2015.

[3] Cole Strangler citing a study by Owen Zidar, "Tax Cuts For The Poor And Middle Class -- Not The Rich -- Create Jobs, Research Shows." Booth School of Economics, *University of Chicago, International Business Times*, April 22, 2015.

limits the stimulus effect because the large tax breaks to the top earners have no measurable effect on the economy.

Trump proposes a large tax cut for the top 1% of taxpayers to stimulate the US economy and create jobs. He is also proposing to do away with the estate tax. Because only tax cuts to the middle class and poor stimulate economic growth. Tax cuts to the rich have no measurable effect.[1]

The top 10% of earners are a relatively small group who do not spend everything they earn. The middle and lower income groups are more numerous and tend to spend everything they earn. A tax cut going to the top earners may well end up in savings while a tax cut to everyone else will almost certainly get spent. This spending stimulates the economy. The Democratic viewpoint on tax cuts is supported by the data.[2]

Clinton's Promises: Clinton takes advantage of the different stimuli to the economy by taxing the wealthy and using the proceeds to stimulate job growth. She also uses generates economic growth by giving tax breaks to the

---

[1] Bruce Bartlett. "Trump's Misguided Embrace of Tax Cuts." *The New York Times*, August 12, 2016.

[2] Ibid.

middle classes. These policies relate in sufficient revenue to reduce national debt by $10 trillion over 10 years.[1]

The Bottom Line: Recent research emphasizes that across the board tax cuts do not stimulate the economy as much as tax cuts targeted at the middle class. Tax policies emphasizing cuts to the wealthy, as Trump's policies do, do not stimulate the economy at all. Trump's policies do add to the deficit, however.[2] Clinton provides tax cuts to the people who will spend their tax savings, the middle class. This will stimulate the economy.   She pays for these tax cuts by increasing taxes on the wealthy.

[1] Cole Strangler citing a study by Owen Zidar, "Tax Cuts For The Poor And Middle Class -- Not The Rich -- Create Jobs, Research Shows." Booth School of Economics, *University of Chicago, International Business Times*, April 22, 2015

[2] Bruce Bartlett, "Trump's Misguided Embrace of Tax Cuts." *The New York Times*, August 12, 2016.

Income Inequality and Growth

Trump: "Do you believe on raising taxes on the wealthy?" Trump was asked on the TODAY Show on Thursday morning. "I do. I do. Including myself. I do"[1]

Clinton: "With all due respect, it is not rich people who made America great. It is the vast American middle class. It is the upward mobility of people who thought they could do better than their parents."[2]

The Issue: From 2009 to 2016, 99% of the increases in income in the U.S. went to the top 1% of Americans.[3] This was not always the case. During the 1950s, 1960s, and 1970s, the earnings of the top 1% grew at the same rate as the earnings of the bottom 99%[4] Many Americans feel that no matter how hard they work, they are getting nowhere,

---

[1] As quoted by Benjy Sarlin, "Donald Trump's tax cuts for top 1% set up general election fight." msnbc.com, April 21, 2016.

[2] As quoted on http://correctrecord.org/the-points/hillary-clinton-a-lifetime-champion-of-income-opportunity/

[3] The average income for the top 1% went up during this persons from $871,100 in 2009 $968,999 in 2013. The average wage for the bottom 99% fell from $44,000 to 43,900. Wolfers is talking about pretax income, so income from social Security and other government programs is not included, but this is the result of our current 'free market' system. See "The Gains From the Economic Recovery Are Still Limited to the Top One Percent", Justin Wolfers, *The New York Times*, January 27, 2015.

[4] "age Stagnation in Nine Charts", Mishel, Gould and Bivens, January 6, 2015. *Economic Policy Institute.* See epi.org.

because they are essentially earning the same income as they did 15 years ago. Because the rich seem to be getting richer at the expense of everyone else, many feel our economic system is rigged.

Economist Dean Baker concludes that wage inequality is caused by the wealthy rigging the US economic system to their own advantage.[1] Top CEOs, venture capitalists and those with inherited wealth contribute in sufficient amounts to political campaigns to gain privileged access. They lobby for legislation which helps them earn more and keep more. This does not generate new income as a new product would, it generates a transfer of income from those who do not have special tax breaks (us) to those who do (the rich).

Economists have evidence that the rising income inequality "is now a significant barrier to economic growth and full employment," because most consumers do not make enough to spend and stimulate the economy.[2] The OECD estimates that the growing income inequality in the US has hampered economic growth by 0.3% in each year

[1] Working Paper: The Upward Redistribution of Income: Are Rents the Story?, Dean Baker, Center for Economic and Policy Research, December, 2015.

[2] Barry Z. Cynamon and Steven M. Fazzari, European Journal of Economics Vol 12 No.2, 2015, Rising inequality and stagnation in the US economy.

for the past 20.[1] The wealthy have access to Congress and bias the tax system to pay far less than they did in the decades after World War II, because they've bent the rules of some system to shuttle more compensation their way."[2] Research by economist Dean Baker asserts that this type of manipulation can account for the majority of the income inequality we have seen over the past several decades.[3]

Trump's Promises: Trump's rhetoric in his speeches is quite different from his written tax proposal on his website. He proposes massive tax cuts on the rich, which will only worsen income inequality. He would give a tax cut of 11.8% to the top 1% of taxpayers, but only a cut of .9% to the bottom 20% of taxpayers.[4]   His deeds go against his populist words.   Worse, his tax plan would make income inequality, and therefore economic stagnations, worse.

---

[1] Income Inequality Hurts Economic Growth, Erik Sherman, Forbes, Dec 9, 2014.

[2] Jim Tankersley, "A big-shot venture capitalist", *Wonkblog*, *The Washington Post*, January 14, 20016.

[3] Working Paper: The Upward Redistribution of Income: Are Rents the Story?, Dean Baker, Center for Economic and Policy Research, December, 2015.

[4] Benjy Sarlin, "Donald Trump's tax cuts for top 1% set up general election fight." *msnbc.com*, April 21, 2016.

Clinton's Promises: Clinton raises taxes on the wealthy to pay for targeted tax cuts and stimulus programs for the middle class. She sets her measure of success as "how much incomes rise for the middle class."[1] If her plan works as advertised, and if she can get Congress to pass it, it would help reduce income inequality in the U.S.

The Bottom Line: Trump's tax and stimulus policies will only make income inequality worse. He may increase economic activity, but most of the new income will go to the wealthy. He may create more jobs for robots than for people.

Clinton targets her tax cuts to help people adjust to job losses and to help them train and find new work. Her stimulus programs are designed to create real jobs not more robots.

---

[1] Quoted from a speech on June 22, 2016 on her web page: https://www.hillaryclinton.com/issues/an-economy-that-works-for-everyone/

Regulating Big Banks: the Dodd Frank Bill

Trump: "Dodd-Frank has made it impossible for bankers to function."[1]

Clinton: "As president, I would not only veto any legislation that would weaken financial reform, but I would also fight for tough new rules, stronger enforcement and more accountability that go well beyond Dodd-Frank."[2]

The Issue: the Clinton Administration, with strong support from the Republican Congress, repealed the Glass - Stiegel Act in 1999. This eliminated the distinction between 'banking' where an institution accepted deposits and made loans, and 'trading' where an institution could speculate on stocks and bonds for itself or on behalf of its clients. Clinton's reforms meant banks and near banks could now speculate on stocks using depositors funds as guaranties. They soon developed clever ways of turning stable, old fashioned mortgages into exciting stocks with good returns - and higher risk - the so-called collateralized debt obligations (CDOs). The Dodd-Frank Act, passed by the Obama Administration in 2010, put controls on these and other risky

[1] "Donald Trump Says He Would Dismantle Dodd-Frank Wall Street Regulation", *Reuters* as quoted in *Fortune*, May 18, 2016.

[2] Where Clinton and Trump Stand on Wall Street", Donna Borak and Henry Williams, *The Wall Street Journal*, June 20, 2016.

activities, gave consumers more rights and protections, and made large banks - those 'too big to fail' (so called because if they failed they would cause a depression, so the government has to bail them out), maintain higher capital balances. Republicans in Congress have been lobbied hard by Wall Street to lessen the controls of the Dodd-Frank Act, and have in some cases been successful.[1]

Trump's Promises: Trump promises to undo the Dodd-Frank Act which he maintains has so much regulation that it is hurting the economy. This would ultimately mean Wall Street might be back where it was before Dodd-Frank was passed and be relatively free to pursue their former activities.[2]

Clinton's Promises: Clinton favors the controls put on the banks by the Dodd Frank bill but promises to extend controls to hedge funds and other types of non-banking financial institutions. She will impose a 'risk tax' on the banks, hedge funds and other institutions larger than $50 billion, to discourage hazardous behavior. She intends to provide independent, non-political funding to the Securities

---

[1] For an excellent overview of this issue, see Mike Collins, "The Big Bank Bailout." *Forbes*, July 14, 2015.

[2] "Donald Trump Says He Would Dismantle Dodd-Frank Wall Street Regulation." *Reuters* as quoted in *Fortune*, May 18, 2016.

and Exchange Commission and the Commodity Futures Trading Commission so they can act independent of political pressure. When a financial institution breaks the law, Clinton pledges to fine the guilty executives personally as well as their institutions. She maintains these policies will make the U.S. economy more stable and help prevent a repeat of the Great Recession of 2009.[1]

The Bottom Line: By most accounts the Dodd-Frank Act has achieved some, but not all of its goals. Large banks are better capitalized, though not smaller. The Volker Rule, separating banking activity from trading activity has gone into effect. But the large banks of the Great Recession are even larger today.[2] Clinton would extend the intent of Dodd Frank making it more effective and applicable to more financial institutions. Trump would turn back the clock and allow the very activities which caused the great recession. of 2007.

---

[1] Hillary Clinton, "Hillary Clinton: How I'd Rein In Wall Street." *The New York Times*, December 7, 2016. Also see: https://www.hillaryclinton.com/issues/wall-street/

[2] Suzanne McGee, "Two cheers for the Dodd-Frank Act – but Wall Street culture needs radical change." *The Guardian*, July 19, 2015.

The Social Safety Net

Food Stamps and Welfare

Trump: "The secret to the 1996 Welfare Reform Act's success was that it tied welfare to work. To get your check, you had to prove that you were enrolled in job-training or trying to find work. Benefits should have strings attached to them. After all, if it's our money recipients are getting, we the people should have a say in how it's spent."[1]

Clinton: "I am concerned about what's happening in every community in America, and that includes white communities, where we are seeing an increase in alcoholism, addiction, earlier deaths. I'm going to do everything I can to address distressed communities, whether they are communities of color, whether they are white communities. I particularly appreciate the proposal that Congressman Jim Clyburn has--the 10-20-30 proposal--to spend more federal dollars in communities with generational poverty."[2]

The Issue: Since 44% of all U.S. children live in poor families and since poverty has a direct affect on educational attainment, poverty is a pressing national issue if the U.S. is going to remain competitive in the international economy.[3]

---

[1] Donald Trump, Time to Get Tough, p.116, Regnery Publishing, 2011.

[2] "Hillary Clinton on Welfare & Poverty", *OnTheIssues*, quoted from a speech delivered by Clinton on February 11, 2016 at the *PBS* Debate.

[3] From the *National Center for Children in Poverty* website. See: http://www.nccp.org/topics/childpoverty.html.

Poverty has been associated with a rise in drug addiction and early deaths.[1]

There are several U.S. government programs that fall under the heading 'welfare'. They include the Supplemental Nutritional Assistance Program (SNAP) formerly known as food stamps, federal unemployment insurance (the FUTA deduction on your paycheck), Medicaid (a federal government insurance program for citizens of all ages whose income is insufficient for healthcare), Temporary Assistance for Need Families (TANF), Women, Infants and Children (WIC), tax credits for working families, and Social Security are the main programs that could be termed 'welfare'.

Republicans question whether the recipients of these programs are truly needy or just lazy. They question whether the poor use their benefits from these programs to avoid work, and whether the monies spent on these programs pass a cost/benefits test.[2]

---

[1] "Hillary Clinton on Welfare & Poverty", *OnTheIssues*, quoted from a speech delivered by Clinton on February 11, 2016 at the *PBS* Debate.

[2] See Paul Ryan's ideas summarized at 'On the Issues'. Go to: http://www.ontheissues.org/House/Paul_Ryan_Welfare_+_Poverty.htm

Democrats point out that 5% of U.S. citizens are poor by third world standards,[1] and that most of the recipients of welfare are working full time.[2]   In their view, the programs which make up modern welfare are inadequate. 41% of the people who received benefits in 2010 under the Supplemental Nutrition Assistance Program (SNAP), the official name for food stamps, live in households with earnings from work. Since one-half of the recipients were under the age of 18 and 8% were over the age of 60, it seems that over half of those able to work, are working.[3] Forcing them to work more (a second job? overtime?) does not seem to be a viable solution.   These families are working full time and not making enough to consistently go without hunger.[4]

Trump's Promises: Trump follows Republican orthodoxy on food stamps and welfare programs.   He states, "That's what I find so morally offensive about welfare

---

[1] Michelle Goldberg, "I Agreed That He Should Sign It." *Slate*, June 6, 2016.

[2] Danielle Johnson, "7 Lies About Welfare That Many People Believe Are Fact." *Groundswell*, March 30, 2015.

[3] Danielle Kurtzleben, "Gingrich's "Uncomfortable Facts" about Food Stamps Hold Water", *US News*, January 17, 2012.

[4] Danielle Johnson, "7 Lies About Welfare That Many People Believe Are Fact." *Groundswell*, March 30, 2015.

dependency: it robs people of the chance to improve."[1] Trump would reduce the current welfare programs and increase the work requirements.

Clinton's Promises: Clinton supports a minimum wage of $15 per hour for urban areas and $12.50 an hour for rural areas.[2] For those with a job, but not able to afford the basics, a raise in the minimum wage would alleviate the worst of the issues around poverty. It would affect 40% of American workers.[3] It would address a basic problem in U.S. society. Many who are working full time cannot afford their basic needs. Clinton would like to extend the current time limit on many welfare programs and increase the effectiveness of the educational programs.[4]

The Bottom Line: Trump is looking for reasons to downsize current welfare programs to reduce a culture of dependence. Clinton wants to change the structure of current welfare programs to make it more effective. She is

[1] Time to Get Tough, p.107, Donald Trump, Regnery Publishing, 2011.

[2] "Hillary Clinton Finally Explains What It Would Take for Her to Support a $15 Minimum Wage", Jordan Weissmann, *Slate*, April 19,2016.

[3] "Hillary Clinton Finally Explains What It Would Take for Her to Support a $15 Minimum Wage", Jordan Weissmann, *Slate*, April 19,2016.

[4] "Interview with Hillary Clinton, Andrea Bernstein, WYNC News, April 15, 2016.

looking for ways to create direct subsidies to poor families with children, such as raising the minimum wage. Clinton's programs address the issue of poverty; Trump views poverty as laziness.

Affordable Care Act (ObamaCare)

Trump: "Completely repeal Obamacare. Our elected representatives must eliminate the individual mandate. No person should be required to buy insurance unless he or she wants to.[1]

Democratic Position: I will, ".. defend and expand the Affordable Care Act, which covers 20 million people".[2]

The Issue: The Republican Congress has voted over 60 times to repeal of the Affordable Healthcare Act (ACA).[3] They object to the penalty imposed on individuals (the individual mandate), to 'cadillac' taxes levied on the wealthy and businesses, and to the administrative burden on healthcare businesses.[4]

The Democrats maintain that the ACA has been very good to consumers. It has abolished pre-existing conditions, provided a means for students to remain on their parents'

---

[1] From Trump's website. See: https://www.donaldjtrump.com/positions/healthcare-reform

[2] From Clinton's website: See: https://www.hillaryclinton.com/issues/health-care/

[3] Deidre Walsh, "House sends Obamacare repeal bill to White House." *CNN*, January 6, 2016

[4] Amy Payne, "Top 5 Reasons to Repeal Obamacare", *The Foundry*, July 11, 2012.

healthcare, provided coverage to over 20 million people, and helped slowdown the growth in healthcare spending. It has not interfered with job growth and has not caused the deficit to explode as predicted by Republicans.[1]

While opposition to the ACA is along party lines, and while the law has not had the disastrous effects predicted by the Republicans, some areas of the country have seen substantial premium increases in the plans presented. These increases and the mandates imposed upon individuals and businesses will continue to make the ACA unpopular. Until Congress can work in a bipartisan fashion to fix problems with the ACA, it will likely remain controversial.[2]

Trump's Promises: Trump would like to revamp the U.S. healthcare system. He starts by repealing the Affordable Care Act, by allowing people to purchase health policies across state lines, by providing more tax deductions for health care, by requiring more transparency from insurance companies. Trump would provide Medicaid

---

[1] Paul Krugman, "Hooray for Obamacare." *The New York Times*, June 25, 2015.

[2] For a summary of the rise in premiums in 2015, see Luke Hilgemann, "Obamacare Premiums Are On The Rise, But Don't Blame Insurers." *Forbes*, December 8, 2015.

through block grants to the states and remove red tape inhibiting drug providers from offering safe, reliable but less expensive products.[1]

Clinton's Promises: Clinton wants to build on the Affordable Care Act which she says does not go far enough. Her policies include lowering the cost of prescription drugs, lowering co-pays and deductibles, expanding Medicaid to all states, providing illegal immigrants with healthcare, expanding access to rural citizens.[2]

The Bottom Line: By repealing the ACA, Trump reintroduces 'pre-existing conditions', removes the portability of plans, and removes the ability to keep a family member on your health insurance until age 26. None of these benefits from the ACA are included in Trump's proposals for a new healthcare system. Trump's policies would effectively take 20 million people off affordable healthcare. Trump does not offer a means to pay for his plan.

Clinton preserves the 'pre-existing condition' benefit, portability, and the ability to keep family member to age 26

---

[1] These points are taken from Trump's website. For a more detailed discussion, see: https://www.donaldjtrump.com/positions/healthcare-reform

[2] From Clinton's website: See: https://www.hillaryclinton.com/issues/health-care/

by keeping the ACA. She would expand existing programs to better cover the poor. Clinton's plans, unlike Trump's, are largely paid for.

Planned Parenthood's Federal Funding

Trump: "Planned Parenthood does some very good work. But I would defund as long as they're doing abortions."[1]

Clinton: "I've been proud to stand with Planned Parenthood for a long time, and as president, I will always have your back."[2]

The Issue: The issue is whether to provide Planned Parenthood with federal funding. Planned Parenthood provides a range of healthcare services to women, including abortions. It receives federal money for its healthcare services to poor women, but no funds from the U.S. government for abortions. Planned Parenthood estimates that less than 7% of its work is for abortions.[3] Conservatives do not want any federal funds going to an organization which provides abortions. Defenders of Planned Parenthood point out that there is no other organization in a position to handle the healthcare needs of the large numbers of poor women. Defunding Planned

---

[1] Dr. Susan Berry, "Donald Trump: 'I Would Defund Planned Parenthood As Long As They're Doing Abortions." *Breitbart*, February 22, 2016.

[2] Sarah Ferris, "Clinton makes pitch to female voters." *The Hill*, June 10, 2016.

[3] Michelle Ye Hee Lee, "For Planned Parenthood abortion stats, '3 percent' and '94 percent' are both misleading," *The Washington Post*, August 12, 2015.

Parenthood will leave large numbers of women without affordable healthcare.

Trump's Promises. Trump says that Planned Parenthood has done "very good work for millions of women". Despite this acknowledgement Trump will not provide federal funds to the organization as long as they are doing abortions.[1]

Clinton's Promises: Clinton has been a long supporter of Planned Parenthood and of a woman's right to determine for herself whether an abortion is needed. She pledges to support all federal funding of Planned Parenthood, to protect 'personal health decisions' made by women, and links these policies to the Affordable Care Act and legislation confronting violence against women.

The Bottom Line. Trump will not support federal funding for Planned Parenthood or any other organization providing abortions. Clinton will fund Planned Parenthood and other organizations providing health care for women.

---

[1] Danielle Paquette, "Donald Trump's incredibly bizarre relationship with Planned Parenthood." *The Washington Post*, March 2, 2016.

Gun Control

Trump: "It's too bad that some of the young people that were killed over the weekend [in Orlando, FL] didn't have guns attached to their (hip), frankly, where bullets could have flown in the opposite direction."[1]

Clinton: "…weapons of war have no place on our streets."[2]

The Issue: More than 30,000 people are killed by firearms each year in the U.S. One-half are between the ages of 18 and 35. One-third are under the age of 20. Homicide is the second leading cause of death among 15-24 year-olds; the primary cause of death among African Americans of that age group. Firearms are regulated by both State and Federal codes which vary considerably. Some states require a license to own a gun and others allow 'open carry' which allows citizens to carry firearms openly visible.[3] Regardless of existing laws, it is generally

---

[1] Trump on the Howie Carr Show as quoted by the *Washington Times*, June 20, 2016.

[2] See: https://www.hillaryclinton.com/issues/gun-violence-prevention/

[3] See: https://en.wikipedia.org/wiki/Gun_laws_in_the_United_States_by_state which provides a state by state rundown of current gun laws.

true that an individual can purchase a firearm at a gun show or online without any sort of background check.[1]

Trump Promises: Trump's policy is to deregulate all purchases of firearms in the U.S. By way of explanations here is an excerpt from Trump's website:

> "Several years ago there was a tremendous program in Richmond, Virginia called Project Exile. It said that if a violent felon uses a gun to commit a crime, you will be prosecuted in federal court and go to prison for five years – no parole or early release. Obama's former Attorney General, Eric Holder, called that a "cookie cutter" program. That's ridiculous. I call that program a success. Murders committed with guns in Richmond decreased by over 60% when Project Exile was in place – in the first two years of the program alone, 350 armed felons were taken off the street."[2]

Clinton's Promises: Clinton's proposes to expand background checks to close the gun show loophole, make 'combat' weapons illegal without a special permit, and restrict domestic abusers and the mentally ill from owning

---

[1] For a detailed discussion on the 'gun show loophole', see PolitiFact: http://www.politifact.com/truth-o-meter/article/2016/jan/07/politifact-sheet-3-things-know-about-gun-show-loop. For a discussion of online guns sales, see: http://www.politifact.com/truth-o-meter/statements/2016/jan/05/barack-obama/obama-violent-felons-can-buy-guns-online-without-b/

[2] See https://www.donaldjtrump.com/positions/second-amendment-rights

guns.   Clinton also pledges to take on the gun lobby by repealing laws which limit manufacturer's liability.[1]

The Bottom Line: 90% of Americans want to see controls on combat weapons and background checks for casual sales.[2] Clinton's proposals address these concerns.

---

[1] From Clinton's website. See: https://www.hillaryclinton.com/issues/gun-violence-prevention/

[2] Lauren Carroll, "Laura Ingraham wrongly says claim that 90% support for gun background checks has been debunked", *PunditFact*, January 5, 2016.

Student Debt

Trump: "the federal government should not be in the business of originating student loans ... and private sector participation in student financing should be restored." - GOP Party Platform[1]

Clinton: " Hillary Clinton has a plan to help millions of Americans with their debt right now, and a plan to make college debt-free for future generations."[2]

The Issue: Total student debt is more than $1.2 trillion. This is more than credit card debt, car loan debt and home equity debt. It is the second largest category of consumer debt. Tuition has risen 40% over the past ten years for a four year degree from a public college. This holds graduates back from forming families, owning homes and forming businesses. [3] Yet parents want to ensure that their children do well in life. College graduates earn 84% more than high

---

[1] "Donald Trump's college plan needs to go back to school", *Moneywatch, CBS News*, July 22, 2016.

[2] From HillaryClinton.com. See: https://www.hillaryclinton.com/briefing/factsheets/2016/07/06/hillary-clintons-commitment-a-debt-free-future-for-americas-graduates/

[3] Ibid.

school graduates over their lifetimes, even when the cost of school debt is factored in.[1]

Trump's Promises. Trump wants to abolish 'most' of the Department of Education which administers Pell Grants, one of the lifelines of poor students for college tuition. Although he has not elaborated, eliminating these loans would be a blow to many students.

In addition, Trump has stated, "the federal government should not be in the business of originating student loans. Private sector participation in student financing should be restored."[2] This would put the student loan program back on the basis that it was on during the Bush administration where it was much more expensive for the students taking out the loans.

Clinton's Promises: Clinton is calling for a three month "moratorium on student debt" to give millions of borrowers fast relief. During the three months students would be given

---

[1] Statistic taken from the U.S. Department of Education found on the study.com website: http://study.com/articles/
How_Much_More_Do_College_Graduates_Earn_Than_Non-College_Graduates.html

[22] "Donald Trump's college plan needs to go back to school", *Money Watch*, *CBS News*, July 22, 2016.

resources to help them restructure their loans, consolidate loans, and sign up for income-based repayment plans.[1]

Clinton also offers a five point plan to help students with their loans in the future. She proposes a new way to refinance loans with savings of up to $2000 per loan, to continue Obama's income based repayment plan, to ask employers to contribute to student debt relief, to defer payments for entrepreneurs starting new businesses, and to reward students who go into public service for two years or more with loan forgiveness.[2]

The Bottom Line. There is a marked difference in the approach towards student loans between Trump and Clinton. Trump views college as an individual privilege and emphasizes a student's responsibility in paying off any loans he or she undertakes. Clinton views a college education more as a public good, such as an effective transportation system, and is looking for ways to help as many students as possible to get a college degree. Clinton's plan is more comprehensive, better thought through and potentially more effective than Trump's plan. Her plan has the potential to

---

[11] From HillaryClinton.com. See: https://www.hillaryclinton.com/briefing/factsheets/2016/07/06/hillary-clintons-commitment-a-debt-free-future-for-americas-graduates/

[2] Ibid.

provide real assistance to college students, whereas Trump's plan, such as it is, does not.

Climate Change

Trump: ""The concept of global warming was created by and for the Chinese in order to make U.S. manufacturing non-competitive."[1]

Clinton: "Lead the world in the fight against climate change by bringing greenhouse gas emissions to 30 percent below what they were in 2005 within the next decade."

The Issue: The Obama Administration views climate change as a serious national threat.   Obama signed the Paris Climate Accords in Paris in 2015 and pledged to reduce emissions tin the United States to levels of 1990. The Administration, through the Environmental Protection Agency, has also issued a series of ruling prohibiting coal burning plants from spewing forth pollutants.   Environmentalists have praised the Obama Administration but claim it has not gone far enough.   Conservatives, most of whom reject climate change as a real threat, call Obama's policies unnecessary red tape which inhibits economic growth.

Trump's Promises: Trump, backed by numerous elected Republican Congressmen, has denounced climate

---

[1] Louis Jacobson, "Yes, Donald Trump did call climate change a Chinese hoax." *PolitiFact,* June 3, 2016. Trump later said this was a joke, but he does call climate change a 'hoax'. See: http://www.politifact.com/truth-o-meter/statements/2016/jun/03/hillary-clinton/yes-donald-trump-did-call-climate-change-chinese-h/

change as a 'hoax'. If elected, he promises to undo President Obama's regulations on electrical generation plants, remove the US from the Paris Climate Accords and give privileged tax treatment to the petroleum industry to encourage drilling. These actions will remove the United States from the group of nations who wish to address climate change.[1]

Clinton's Promises: Clinton, if elected, would build and expand on President Obama's efforts to address climate change. and aim to make "the United States the world's clean energy superpower."[2] This would not only involve opposing Republican efforts to undo Obama's Clean Power Plan in Congress and the Courts, but proposing her own Clean Energy Challenge, "a broad federal program that would partner with states, cities, and rural communities on renewable energy, power grid resilience, and air pollution control.[3]

---

[1] Justin Worland, "Donald Trump Promises to Cut Regulation on 'Phony' Environmental Issues." *Time*, May 26, 2016.

[2] "Campaign 2016: The Candidates and the World." *The Council on Foreign Relations,* as of July 15, 2016. See: http://www.cfr.org/campaign2016/hillary-clinton/on-energy-and-climate

[3] For more details, see: https://www.hillaryclinton.com/briefing/factsheets/2015/07/26/renewable-power-vision/

The Bottom Line: The difference between Trump and Clinton on climate change could not be more stark. Trump would undo Obama's programs, including U.S. commitments in the Paris Climate Accords, and attempt to stimulate oil and gas drilling in the United States. Clinton would expand controls on drilling and pollution and make a concerted effort to stimulate alternative energy solutions for their impact on the climate and for their business revenues.

About the Author

Carl Widell was a Republican for 30 years. When he saw Republican administrations run up huge deficits he concluded the Democrats were more responsible and switched parties. He has served as chair of the Talbot County (MD) Democratic Party, ran the 2012 Obama campaign in nine counties, was an alternate to the 2012 Democratic Convention, and has served on the Talbot County School Board.

After having started and run several software companies, Carl has become involved in public/private development projects in West Africa in the petroleum and water treatment industries.

Carl lives in St. Michaels with his architect wife, Pamela Heyne, and his two daughters Svetlana and Katya.

www.ingramcontent.com/pod-product-compliance
Lightning Source LLC
Chambersburg PA
CBHW050405290526
45786CB00003B/1137